Savor Communion

Bob Perry & Amy Joy Lykosh

Amy Joy Lykosh
Bob Perry

MAKARIOS
PRESS

Esmont, VA

Makarios Press
P.O. Box 28, Esmont, VA 22937

Scripture in NIV unless otherwise stated.

Cover & Design: Nate Braxton

ISBN 978-1-956561-17-3

Printed in the United States of America

CONTENTS

INTRODUCTION

In October 2021, Bob Perry and I led our community in Savor Communion, a 31 day challenge to take communion (also called the Table of the Lord or the Eucharist) every day.

Most of us do not belong to a community that meets daily, so to take communion every day required the shift to partake alone, or with a spouse or a friend.

Before we started, as we talked about this idea with our family and friends, we had two responses: "Wow, that sounds really powerful!" And, "Wow! That sounds really controversial!" (Sometimes followed with, "What do you think about _____?")

It should go without saying that if this goes against your conscience, please do not participate. *Never do anything against your conscience!*

But if you're excited, or cautiously curious, or even terribly skeptical ... welcome!

Below you'll find some of the questions and answers that we have wrestled through.

We talked and prayed in the months before October, planning how to invite our community to partake of the Table of the Lord.

At the end of August, as we asked the Lord to reveal more of himself to us, Bob suddenly gasped. "I've been praying that

I would have a deeper knowledge of the Table of the Lord since 1990 or 1991. That's 30 years!"

For 30 years, he's been praying for more.

And one of the standout characteristics of Bob is: he prays effective prayers.

We are so excited to bring *Savor Communion* to you.

We bless you to continue to participate in the Table of the Lord in your own community, in whatever way you already do. And we invite you to participate in new ways as well, as you'll see in these pages.

— *Bob & Amy*

INTRODUCTORY REFLECTIONS

Reflection 1
HOLDING THINGS IN TENSION: THE WAY OF WISDOM

Have you ever come across dueling scriptures?

Like Proverbs 26:4-5: "Do not answer a fool according to his folly, or you yourself will be just like him. Answer a fool according to his folly, or he will be wise in his own eyes."

And you think ... hmmm. Do not answer? Answer? Which is it?

Of course, the answer is: wisdom discerns what to do in each situation. Life isn't a grid of boxes to check ("Answer every fool: check!"), but relational, complex, full of things held in tension.

For some time, I've been wrestling with this idea of communion as another thing held in tension: something that's holy, but also earthly, and how we hold both.

The communion elements themselves, when Jesus gave them to the disciples, weren't special. He didn't have the matzoh on a gold-rimmed plate. He didn't drink the wine out of a special crystal goblet.

He used what he had in hand already, during the

Passover meal.

And he made the earthly elements holy.

Jesus came into the real world and lived in the midst of the dust and the need.

And yet, somehow this meal, this *communion*, which he meant as a point of connection, becomes a point of division and contention.

Strategically, why do you think that is?

Reflection 2
PROCLAIM THE LORD'S DEATH

In a time of war, does the general seek to take out sparsely populated rural communities or military and industrial hubs? (Just in case you're not sure: military and industrial hubs.)

The New Testament is clear that we have an enemy. (Not human! "For our struggle is not against flesh and blood, but against the rulers, against the authorities, against the powers of this dark world and against the spiritual forces of evil in the heavenly realms."[1])

When enemies seek to overthrow you, if they can shut down your most strategic weapons, they gain the advantage.

So ... let's talk about communion.

When Paul wrote about the Table of the Lord, he said, "For whenever you eat this bread and drink this cup, you proclaim the Lord's death until he comes."

That word "proclaim," in the Greek, is *katangello*.

Katangello means declare, preach, make known, proclaim publicly.[2]

When you eat this bread and drink this cup, you declare, preach, make known, proclaim publicly.

The Table of the Lord is not a quiet, introspective moment,

but a loud statement.

Strategically, if you were the enemy, then, and wanted to prevent the proclamation of the Lord's death, you could do it in a few ways.

You could distract the followers of Christ from the main point (proclaiming Christ's death!), and entice them to engage in disagreements over the meaning, the transmission, the proper form.

You could stir up controversy and animosity around a simple act, creating a lot of tension instead of fellowship.

You could make the logistics seem challenging enough that many believers only proclaim once a month ... or once a quarter.

Is it possible that all the controversy through the centuries has shut down one of the most powerful tools that Jesus gave to his followers?

Without diving in to the specifics of the disagreement ... do you see at least the possibility that these distractions, controversies, and logistical challenges might be an effective flanking attempt?

Reflection 3

DIVE DEEPER INTO WHAT YOU ALREADY KNOW

Bob and his wife went to a week-long retreat on the Father's heart.

Having met them both, I thought they both already had a good sense of the heart of the Father. Far better than most people I've met. They understood the love of God and already lived from that place of love and sonship.

But Bob came back saying, "I know more. I understand more deeply the Father's heart."

I thought, *Wow. So there is always more to be learned.*

Even what seems like a simple concept—like *sonship*, like *love*—I wonder now if they always have more levels to explore.

After all, as a child, we understand what it means to be a child. As an adult, we have a better understanding of the challenges of parenting (and even of what it would have been like to parent ourselves!).

Likewise with God: we start off, and know him. But then, as we walk with him longer, we learn more about his love for us. We understand in greater measure what it is to be his child.

C.S. Lewis, in *The Last Battle*, had the line, "Further up and further in"—come deeper into the truths, deeper into the reality.

I've been thinking about the unexplored depths of communion.

Because as a consistent church-going Christian, I've taken communion since childhood. And before every time of partaking, we would be brought back into remembrance of the death of Christ.

And this seems, in many ways, straightforward.

But I think that the Lord has even more for us in the Table of the Lord, in the Meal of the Messiah.

Reflection 3
COMMUNION AS A SYMBOL

For those who eat and drink without discerning the body of Christ eat and drink judgment on themselves. That is why many among you are weak and sick, and a number of you have fallen asleep.[3]
Based on Paul's teaching, I don't take communion lightly. None of us should.

As Paul said in the familiar passage: For I received from the Lord what I also passed on to you: *The Lord Jesus, on the night he was betrayed, took bread, and when he had given thanks, he broke it and said, "This is my body, which is for you; do this in remembrance of me." In the same way, after supper he took the cup, saying, "This cup is the new covenant in my blood; do this, whenever you drink it, in remembrance of me." For whenever you eat this bread and drink this cup, you proclaim the Lord's death until he comes.*[4]

At the end of his life here on Earth, Jesus offered his disciples his body and blood.

At that time, he wasn't literally offering his body and blood. His body hadn't yet been broken, nor his blood spilled out. He was not yet glorified.

He was speaking metaphorically. And yet communion is not just a symbol.

A symbol is a representation of something else, like the cross is a reminder of Jesus.

But, clearly, Paul never wrote to any of the churches to say, "Some of you are wearing a cross as a necklace, and shoving it under your pillow at night, which is pretty disrespectful, and as a result, some of you have died."

Clearly, communion is on a different level.

Historically, the church calls it a sacrament, defined as "a religious ceremony or ritual regarded as imparting divine grace."[5]

I wasn't entirely sure what "divine grace" meant. Wikipedia says, "the divine influence which operates in humans to regenerate and sanctify, to inspire virtuous impulses, and to impart strength to endure trial and resist temptation; and as an individual virtue or excellence of divine origin."[6]

Again, I'm not sure of all of the theological implications of all of those words, nor what controversies these ideas may have had through the centuries.

But clearly communion *does* something.

Reflection 4

THE LORD'S TABLE IN THE GOSPELS

The three Synoptic Gospels (Matthew, Mark, and Luke) all tell the story of the Last Supper in the Scripture. Take a few minutes to read through them.

Matthew and Mark's accounts are almost identical, with just a few words different between them. Luke changes the order around.

Matthew 26:26-29

While they were eating, Jesus took bread, and when he had given thanks, he broke it and gave it to his disciples, saying, "Take and eat; this is my body."

Then he took a cup, and when he had given thanks, he gave it to them, saying, "Drink from it, all of you. This is my blood of the covenant, which is poured out for many for the forgiveness of sins. I tell you, I will not drink from this fruit of the vine from now on until that day when I drink it new with you in my Father's kingdom."

Mark 14:22-25

While they were eating, Jesus took bread, and when he had given thanks, he broke it and gave it to his disciples, saying, "Take it; this is my body."

Then he took a cup, and when he had given thanks, he gave it to them, and they all drank from it.

"This is my blood of the covenant, which is poured out for many," he said to them. "Truly I tell you, I will not drink again from the fruit of the vine until that day when I drink it new in the kingdom of God."

Luke 22:14-21

When the hour came, Jesus and his apostles reclined at the table. And he said to them, "I have eagerly desired to eat this Passover with you before I suffer. For I tell you, I will not eat it again until it finds fulfillment in the kingdom of God."

After taking the cup, he gave thanks and said, "Take this and divide it among you. For I tell you I will not drink again from the fruit of the vine until the kingdom of God comes."

And he took bread, gave thanks and broke it, and gave it to them, saying, "This is my body given for you; do this in remembrance of me."

In the same way, after the supper he took the cup, saying, "This cup is the new covenant in my blood, which is poured out for you. But the hand of him who is going to betray me is with mine on the table."

———•❈•———

The apostle John talks about this meal, but doesn't mention the bread and the wine specifically.

Here's the story John tells, during a scene when the disciples were trying to figure out who would betray Jesus.

John 13:26-30

Jesus answered, "It is the one to whom I will give this piece of bread when I have dipped it in the dish." Then, dipping the piece of bread, he gave it to Judas, the son of Simon Iscariot. As soon as Judas took the bread, Satan entered into him.

So Jesus told him, "What you are about to do, do quickly." But no one at the meal understood why Jesus said this to him. Since Judas had charge of the money, some thought Jesus was telling him to buy what was needed for the festival, or to give something to the poor. As soon as Judas had taken the bread, he went out. And it was night.

———— · ✸ · ————

What was it about the bread that caused Judas to have Satan enter him?

Perhaps because Judas was so intent on betrayal, even though Jesus was extending fellowship? We aren't told.

Reflection 5
THE LORD'S TABLE IN THE EPISTLES

In his epistle, his letter, to the church at Corinth, Paul had a good bit to say about the Lord's Table.

The Corinthians were not using this gathering as a way to grow closer together. Rather, some would treat the time as their own private party: gorging on the bread and wine, while others went hungry.

This is so bizarre, it's hard to believe.

Rather than a celebration of togetherness and unity, instead it was a free-for-all of greed and selfishness. How unbecoming of the children of God!

Paraphrasing Paul: "Hey, you guys, this is really disgusting. You wouldn't do this if you were going to someone's house for dinner! You wouldn't go and eat all of the food and leave none for your host! You wouldn't drink all of the wine and leave others sitting there thirsty! Can you please exercise some better manners? Can you actually partake of this together as a way of building community and communion with one another and with God? Don't come hungry! Here's what the Lord taught me. The Table of the Lord is a time to remember Jesus's death. Don't partake without remembering Christ."

Here's the whole passage.

In the following directives I have no praise for you, for your meetings do more harm than good. In the first place, I hear that when you come together as a church, there are divisions among you, and to some extent I believe it. No doubt there have to be differences among you to show which of you have God's approval. So then, when you come together, it is not the Lord's Supper you eat, for when you are eating, some of you go ahead with your own private suppers. As a result, one person remains hungry and another gets drunk. Don't you have homes to eat and drink in? Or do you despise the church of God by humiliating those who have nothing? What shall I say to you? Shall I praise you? Certainly not in this matter!

For I received from the Lord what I also passed on to you: The Lord Jesus, on the night he was betrayed, took bread, and when he had given thanks, he broke it and said, "This is my body, which is for you; do this in remembrance of me." In the same way, after supper he took the cup, saying, "This cup is the new covenant in my blood; do this, whenever you drink it, in remembrance of me." For whenever you eat this bread and drink this cup, you proclaim the Lord's death until he comes.

So then, whoever eats the bread or drinks the cup of the Lord in an unworthy manner will be guilty of sinning against the body and blood of the Lord. Everyone ought to examine themselves before they eat of the bread and drink from the cup. For those who eat and drink without discerning the body of Christ eat and drink judgment on themselves. That is why many among you are weak and sick, and a number of you have fallen asleep. But if we were more discerning with regard to ourselves, we would not come under such judgment. Nevertheless, when we are judged in this way by the Lord, we are being disciplined so that we will not be finally condemned with the world.

So then, my brothers and sisters, when you gather to eat, you should all eat together. Anyone who is hungry should eat something at home, so that when you meet together it may not result in judgment.

And when I come I will give further directions.[7]

This passage seems clear enough to me, when read in context.

And yet I know I have heard scores of sermons over the years, warning about not eating and drinking judgment on ourselves by not examining ourselves carefully and coming to the Table without sin.

Which is odd for a few reasons.

First, because the first Table of the Lord was just about Jesus: *This is my body, broken for you. This is my blood, poured out for you.* He didn't instruct the disciples to *examine themselves* before he handed around the bread and the wine.

Second, because the focus seems to be going in the wrong direction. The emphasis I've seen in church so often is on the warning.

But the point from the scriptures is that we're supposed to be proclaiming the Lord's death until he comes, discerning the body of Christ.

Third, because in most modern contexts, people would have no ability to eat and drink to excess. The small wafer, the cup of juice ... these would not be enough to satiate hunger or produce drunkenness.

Reflection 6
MESSED-UP PARTY

On Joe's birthday, he was ready
To blow out the candles when Phil said,
"You know, I have a lot of sin in my life."

I looked in disbelief.
"This is Joe's moment! It's not about you."

"Yes," Phil continued. "Sometimes
I grow irate with pokey drivers on the road.
That's not exactly loving my enemies."

"Can we please talk about this later?"
I pleaded. "Let's let Joe blow out his candles,
And we'll all eat cake."

Completely ignoring me, his melancholy
Diatribe against himself went on,
Covering sins from elementary school on,
While the candle wax pooled in the frosting
And Joe stood, neglected.

None of this actually happened.

But do we do the same thing?
We're invited to a celebration
Of a Son, and instead focus on
Our failures, ignoring the
One
Worthy.

Reflection 7

THE TABLE OF THE LORD AND MAN-MADE RESTRICTIONS

When Jesus gave his disciples the bread and the wine, he said, "Do this, as often as you eat it, in remembrance of me."

At times I have wondered if he meant, "As often as you *eat*." That wouldn't be bad, to remember Christ's death every time we put something in our mouths.

But assuming a more traditional idea, with the bread and the wine, the Table of the Lord, I am astonished at how divisive this sacrament is.

Many churches restrict who is allowed to partake.

- Maybe not enough training. "If you haven't done a three-year study with our church: no."
- Maybe not the right prerequisites: "If you haven't been baptized: no."
- Maybe not the right affiliation. "If you aren't a member of our church: no."
- Maybe not the right company gathered. "If you don't have a priest: no."

But when I look at the New Testament, this doesn't seem

scriptural.

First, Jesus gave the bread and the wine to his disciples. From there, the church spread: first through a large-scale evangelistic outburst, and then mostly person-to-person, house-to-house. Small pockets of believers met in homes, with, at times, just parents and children.

Those homes didn't have a priest or a bishop.

Though the believers were baptized at some point, my understanding is that they weren't always baptized right away.

The early believers didn't have the New Testament yet, so they hardly had a systematized theology.

Denominational affiliations hadn't developed.

And I understand the hesitation about taking communion alone. After all, how is this actually "communion," which is, by one definition, "the sharing or exchanging of intimate thoughts and feelings, especially when the exchange is on a mental or spiritual level; common participation in a mental or emotional experience."

How can you participate in communion, in right fellowship, all by yourself?

Good question! Here are some thoughts.

The New Testament tells us that Christ lives in us.[8] Julian of Norwich said, "God is nearer to us than our own soul."

So ... are we ever actually alone? Even if I partake of communion on my own, I'm not actually alone. I am still participating in the Table of the Lord, in the wider fellowship of saints.

Moreover, as different areas of the world undergo persecution: what does it look like to partake of the Lord's Table if you are the only believer you know?

Worldwide, this isn't unheard of. Not only because some communities have only a few converts, but also because some places are simply dangerous to live.

Would you advise these brothers and sisters never to take communion because they didn't have a larger fellowship to join with them?

How much of this idea of "must participate in a larger group, or not at all" is because of Western church cultural context?

I am sure that, ideally, conversions would happen within entire families, not just to single individuals. But when the ideal doesn't happen ... what then?

Reflection 8

THE ELEMENTS AND THE TABLE OF THE LORD

When Jesus offered the disciples the bread and the wine during communion, these are such lovely symbols. Perhaps the red wine looks a bit like blood; the unleavened matzoh a bit like flesh.

I have heard that some brothers and sisters insist that bread and wine are the only correct elements.

But then this gets a little murky for me.

Most churches I have attended do not actually offer wine, but grape juice.

Yes ... these are both grape products, but wine and juice are not the same thing.

And what if you use white wine instead of red? Then it no longer looks like blood!

And what about the recovering alcoholics? If the church dogmatically insists on wine, then is the recovering alcoholic excluded from this part of the service?

One church I went to offered wine in the inner cups, juice in the outer ring, broken pieces of bread, and gluten-free crackers. They were covering their bases!

I have often attended a service with a lovely yeast bread.

But Jesus broke bread during Passover, when he would have offered only a non-yeast bread. These aren't the same thing.

And what about the gluten-free among us? If the church insists on wheat bread, then is the gluten-free person excluded from this part of the service?

And what about the wheat itself? Modern-day wheat, often genetically modified, and certainly selected over the last 2000 years, is not much like the first century counterpart. Do we need to seek out yeast-free spelt crackers?

What about my friend whose body reacts badly to certain common foods? She eats a salt-free cracker and takes water for her communion. Would you condemn her for that?

But is the point the specific elements? Or remembering the body and blood of the Lord?

Can we unite around Christ, and not be hung up on specific details ... especially since these details vary already?

Here's another line of thought, around the same topic.

My family tried farming for a few years. Pretty much everything we tried failed, but one of the things we learned was that each climate zone, each site, had its own specific specialty for growing.

Similar to site-specific crops, I also believe that Jesus speaks into every ethnic group and cultural context.

One of my favorite missionary stories I heard so long ago that I no longer remember the source, but a man was working with an indigenous culture, one where the men wore nothing but a g-string.

One day a man came to the missionary and said, "Jesus met me on the trail." And he shared whatever word the Lord had given him. I'm sure it was beautiful. And the man turned to go, but the missionary said, "Oh, wait! Can you tell me what was he wearing?"

I thought that was such a practical question. When Jesus spoke to a man in a g-string, did he wear a flowing robe, as in the children's picture Bibles?

The man looked at the missionary as if the missionary had gone soft in the head and said, "He was wearing a g-string ... like me."

Jesus is so beautiful. He goes into every culture.

Agriculturally, then, let me say: wheat and grapes don't grow naturally all over the world. As I understand it, here in Virginia, for several centuries, all grapevines suffered from some virus or other death-inducing issue. Today we have vineyards throughout the state, because they are grafted onto a rootstock that is resistant to that virus.

And so to say to a culture and a place with limited access to the outside world, "You can't take communion unless you import bread, and unless you get some form of grape wine" ... that imposes Western society onto an indigenous culture. It makes communion not universal. It's saying, "Your culture isn't good enough. Unless you import these things at great expense, you cannot participate."

I suspect that God speaks and is content with whatever bread and wine substitute they have in their culture, because Jesus comes into every culture and is so beautiful in every culture. He invites every tribe and language and people and nation to come and celebrate him and his death.

Reflection 9
TAKING COMMUNION: POSSIBLE COMPANIONS

One of my friends asked a beautiful question about communion and children.

I know that many denominations have restrictions for children: what age are young ones allowed to take communion? How much training must they have? Some have a requirement like a confirmation class.

On the surface, this makes sense: prevent people eating without discerning Christ. And since babies and toddlers do not understand what Christ did on the cross, they would bring judgment on themselves if they ate and drank just because they wanted the snack of cracker and juice.

And yet: why would we restrict our children from proclaiming Christ's death?

Thinking again about the first communion, Jesus didn't give any restrictions to the disciples. Luke makes it clear that Judas was sitting at the table, and Jesus didn't say, "Ooohhhh! Judas! Maybe don't partake!"

It's not like there were extra circles of hell waiting for Judas because he partook.

The point is not the punishment! The point is the

remembrance.

"Do this in remembrance of me."

Earlier in Jesus' ministry, Matthew records this story:

Then people brought little children to Jesus for him to place his hands on them and pray for them. But the disciples rebuked them. Jesus said, "Let the little children come to me, and do not hinder them, for the kingdom of heaven belongs to such as these." When he had placed his hands on them, he went on from there.[9]

When the disciples tried to keep the little children from Jesus, he wasn't pleased.

It seems that Jesus actually cares about children.

As the record of all the scriptures also shows: "Children are a heritage from the LORD, offspring a reward from him."[10]

So in general, it would seem that keeping children away from Jesus, from thinking about Jesus and remembering his death, is maybe not the direction that most pleases God.

So how can we include children in the Table of the Lord?

When children are very young, they don't eat solid food. After that, they might be in and out of church, not really paying a whole lot of attention, easy enough perhaps to distract them.

But if you start reading picture Bibles from a young age, usually by the time a child can speak a few words, you could ask, "What did Jesus do?" and they might answer, "Die on the cross for our sins."

"What happened next?"

"He rose again."

As the elements pass around, you can say, "What is the bread?"

"The body of Christ."

"What is the juice?"

"The blood of Christ."

"And we're remembering Jesus' death, right?"

"Right."

For me, that was enough of an understanding to feel

comfortable allowing my children to partake together of the body of Christ with the larger body of Christ.

I wanted them to have that sense of larger community, of being part of something bigger than themselves and their own family.

If you have children still at home with you, consider partaking with them.

Celebrate Christ's death, together.

Christ died for you, and he died for your children, and for your family.

Thanks be to God.

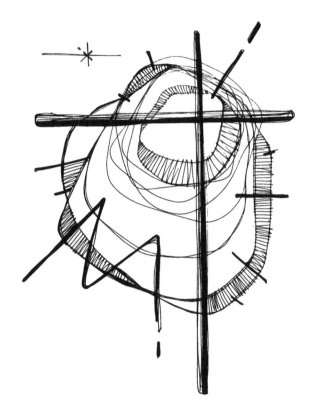

31-DAY
CHALLENGE

Savor Communion: Day 1

FAITHFULNESS AND THE FIRST COMMUNION

Lord, we think of the first communion, and how you gave the bread and the wine to your disciples, knowing that very night, one would betray you, one would deny you, and the other ten would turn away.

We think of how John records that, after eating, the disciples began disputing about which of them was the greatest.

These were the men who partook of the first Lord's Table. And you invited them to fellowship.

Lord Jesus, thank you that you don't look on our worthiness to determine whether we can partake or not. Thank you that you don't deal with us according to our faithfulness. "If we are faithless, he remains faithful, for he cannot disown himself."[11]

Thank you, Jesus, for how beautiful you are.

———•✳•———

For I received from the Lord what I also passed on to you: The Lord Jesus, on the night he was betrayed, took bread, and when he had given thanks, he broke it and said, "This is my body, which is for you; do this in remembrance of me." In the same way, after supper he took the cup, saying, "This cup is the new covenant in my blood; do this, whenever you drink it, in remembrance of me." For whenever you eat this bread and drink this cup, you proclaim the Lord's death until he comes.[12]

———— • ✹ • ————

Thank you, Lord, for the power of the Table of the Lord.
Thank you for the amazing covenant you've made with us.
Lord, it gives us such hope. It gives us such joy.
Thank you for the new covenant. Thank you for your body.
Thank you for your blood. Thank you for the bread, and thank you for the cup.
We eat and drink, in Jesus' name.
Amen.
Let's celebrate!

Savor Communion: Day 2
FELLOWSHIP

Lord, you are so good. Thank you.

We think of how even the name "communion" is another word for "fellowship."

Thank you that as we partake of the Table of the Lord, that we get to fellowship with you and with the saints around the world and throughout history. Thank you that we, too, are living stones in your spiritual house.[13] Thank you that whether we partake alone or with one other person or in a group, that you are always with us.

Thank you for the great privilege you give us to be with you and with one another. You are always the greater giver, and we agree with what James says, that every good and perfect gift is from above, coming down from the Father of the heavenly lights, who does not change like shifting shadows.[14]

The fellowship of the saints counts as one of your good and perfect gifts.

How beautiful you are, Lord.

————— • ✻ • —————

While they were eating, Jesus took bread, and when he had given thanks, he broke it and gave it to his disciples, saying, "Take and eat; this is my body."

Then he took a cup, and when he had given thanks, he gave it to them, saying, "Drink from it, all of you. This is my blood of the covenant, which is poured out for many for the forgiveness of sins."[15]

———— • ❀ • ————

Lord, we speak a blessing over this bread. We speak a blessing over this cup. We speak a blessing, in Jesus' name, a deep friendship with God.

Let's eat and drink and celebrate the Lord's body and blood. Amen!

Thank you, Lord!

Savor Communion: Day 3
THE MOST INTIMATE ACT YOU CAN DO ON YOUR OWN

Lord, when we take in food and drink, it becomes a part of us. It goes into our very cells.

I think of how Joel Salatin said that eating is the most intimate thing you can do outside of the marital act, because you're actually taking something from the outside and bringing it inside of you, so it becomes part of you.

It strikes me, Lord, that you call yourself the bridegroom, and that your church is your bride, but in the way that we haven't actually had the marriage supper of the Lamb yet, thank you that you give us literal, physical bread and wine to bring into ourselves and renew us. Thank you that you give us the opportunity to unite with you spiritually, that you come and live in us, but also that you offer us your body to take in on a cellular level.

Thank you that you are that close to us.

———— • ✻ • ————

While they were eating, Jesus took bread, and when he had given thanks, he broke it and gave it to his disciples, saying, "Take it; this is my body."

Then he took a cup, and when he had given thanks, he gave it to them, and they all drank from it.

"This is my blood of the covenant, which is poured out for many," he said to them. "Truly I tell you, I will not drink again from the fruit of the vine until that day when I drink it new in the kingdom of God."[16]

———— •❀• ————

Lord, as we hold the bread in our hand and hold the cup in our hand, we thank you, Jesus, that you are so good. We thank you that you give us your body and your blood.

Jesus, thank you that the power in your name is supernatural power. Through your righteousness we come and ask that you bless the bread, bless the cup. We remember your death, burial, and resurrection.

Hallelujah!

Let's eat and drink.

Savor Communion: Day 4
DAILY BREAD

Lord, some years ago, in *Eat This Book*, Eugene Peterson wrote about the phrase "daily bread."

For years scholars assumed that this must be some deeply spiritual word, because it wasn't found in other Greek writings.

Then in 1925, in an archaeological dig in a scrapheap in Egypt, they found a shopping list, and it had that same word, "daily bread."

So we ask that you would, indeed, give us this day our daily bread. Don't give us yesterday's bread. Like the manna from heaven, we need your new bread every day.

Thank you, Jesus, that you were so astonishingly earthly. Thank you that you used everyday language, everyday concepts, and gave them new meaning, new power.

So we ask for our daily bread *today*. The new bread of your sustenance. The daily bread that satisfies our hunger and our need. Lord, this is what you taught us to ask for, and so we do.

Thank you, Lord.

———— • ❋ • ————

When the hour came, Jesus and his apostles reclined at the

table. And he said to them, "I have eagerly desired to eat this Passover with you before I suffer. For I tell you, I will not eat it again until it finds fulfillment in the kingdom of God."

After taking the cup, he gave thanks and said, "Take this and divide it among you. For I tell you I will not drink again from the fruit of the vine until the kingdom of God comes."

And he took bread, gave thanks and broke it, and gave it to them, saying, "This is my body given for you; do this in remembrance of me."

In the same way, after the supper he took the cup, saying, "This cup is the new covenant in my blood, which is poured out for you. But the hand of him who is going to betray me is with mine on the table."[17]

———————·✻·———————

Lord, we come in such joy, for communion with you, for fellowship with one another.

Lord, we bless you. Lord, we praise you. Thank you, Lord, for the mystery of the bread, your body. Thank you for the mystery of the cup, your blood. Thank you, Jesus.

We eat and drink in celebration of your death and resurrection.

Amen.

Savor Communion: Day 5
THE BEST WINE

Lord, we think about the first miracle recorded in the book of John, when you turned the water into wine.[18]

In the natural, Lord, the grape vines first need to grow grapes, and then the grapes need to be pressed and the juice fermented.

But you brought about this miracle of instantaneous development.

And you did it for a party where the people were already so tipsy that they wouldn't have been able to taste the difference between mediocre wine and the best wine.

It astonishes us, Lord, that you care so much about celebrations.

You served the best wine at the end.

We think about how you allowed your people, for several thousand years, to grope after you, but then, you came, Jesus, at just the right time, in the fullness of time.

And as you used the wine as the picture of your blood being spilled out and offered for many for the remission of sins, we are so honored that you invite us to partake.

As your first recorded miracle was about how you provided wine for the people for their joy, Lord, that we say thank you

that you continue to do that, that we get to partake of the
wine of your blood for our joy.

Thank you, Jesus.

———— · ✴ · ————

Let me go over with you again exactly what goes on in the
Lord's Supper and why it is so centrally important. I received
my instructions from the Master himself and passed them on
to you. The Master, Jesus, on the night of his betrayal, took
bread. Having given thanks, he broke it and said,

This is my body, broken for you.
Do this to remember me.
After supper, he did the same thing with the cup:
This cup is my blood, my new covenant with you.
Each time you drink this cup, remember me.

What you must solemnly realize is that every time you eat
this bread and every time you drink this cup, you reenact in
your words and actions the death of the Master. You will be
drawn back to this meal again and again until the Master
returns. You must never let familiarity breed contempt.[19]

———— · ✴ · ————

Lord, we think of the bread. Thank you.

And we think of the grapes. We think of the crushing, of
the fermentation, of the process. We think of how you work
all things out.

You're the master. You're the administrator of all, the
creator of all, the designer of all.

And, Lord, as you created this mystery of the bread and the
cup, of communion, Lord, we take a holy pause and say we're
so thankful for you, so thankful for the blood of the new
covenant, the forgiveness of sins. Thank you that all shame
is gone, all striving is gone, that we have no condemnation

because of the blood of the Lamb, the blood of Jesus. So Lord, we take this bread and this cup, and we give thanks. It was given for us. We eat and drink in remembrance of you, Jesus.
  Amen.

Savor Communion: Day 6
COMFORT AND LIGHTNING

Lord, when we think about the bread and the wine, how different these two things are.

Bread is a comfort food, predictable, dependable, faithful. For those exhausted, it's strength and energy. It's stable and delicious.

Wine, though, is less predictable. Even a swallow is enough to feel the warmth into the stomach, as the tongue experiences the flavors, and, perhaps, the body experiences the unexpected loosening of emotions.

Wine is a gift, emphasizing the suddenlies, the breakthroughs, the unexpectedness, the creativity. It's the red of the cardinal in the midst of the greenery—whimsical.

Thank you, Jesus, that you give us both bread and wine.

———— · ✸ · ————

During the meal, Jesus took and blessed the bread, broke it, and gave it to his disciples:

Take, eat.

This is my body.

Taking the cup and thanking God, he gave it to them:

Drink this, all of you.

This is my blood,
God's new covenant poured out for many people for the
forgiveness of sins.[20]

—————— • ❋ • ——————

Thank you, Father.
Thank you, Jesus.
Thank you, Holy Spirit.
Thank you for the beauty of your body, the mystery of the
bread and the wine. Thank you for the power in Jesus' name.
We worship you, Lord. We give you glory. We give you
honor. Amen.
Let's partake and celebrate!

Savor Communion: Day 7
NO STRIVING

Lord, as we think about New Testament people, like Paul and Peter, they seem so task-oriented. And, Lord, we often are task-oriented, too. It gives us comfort that you would choose men like Peter and Paul, because often we, too, like to get things done.

When we come to the Table of the Lord, though, we thank you that we don't come with a sense of, "Work harder, pray harder, intercede harder ... STRIVE!"

Lord, we've tried that before, and the fruit that comes from striving is an incomplete, unhealthy, unhappy heart.

Lord, let us be at peace during the mad rush. Let us follow your rhythm.

Thank you that you invite us to enter your rest.

We want all that you have for us, and we want to accomplish your full purpose, but we want to get there in sync with you.

————— • ✱ • —————

In the course of their meal, having taken and blessed the bread, he broke it and gave it to them.

Then he said,

Take, this is my body.

Taking the chalice, he gave it to them, thanking God, and they all drank from it. He said,
This is my blood,
God's new covenant,
Poured out for many people.
"I'll not be drinking wine again until the new day when I drink it in the kingdom of God."[21]

———— • ❋ • ————

Jesus, we see how you blessed the bread and gave thanks for the cup and shared the bread and the wine with your disciples.
Thank you that you continue to share your body and blood with us.
Amen.
We eat and drink in remembrance of you.

Savor Communion: Day 8

PARTAKING OF THE BODY AND THE BLOOD

Lord, we come to your Table with such thankfulness. Jesus, you invite us to fellowship with you, to enter in to your suffering, and share that with you and with one another.

Lord, when you walked this earth, you used your body for healing and for teaching, for instructing and correcting and blessing.

And, Lord, your blood astonishes us. It justifies us;[22] redeems us, giving us forgiveness of sins;[23] cleanses us from all sin;[24] brings us near to God;[25] defeats the enemy.[26]

Lord, your body and your blood give us the way to live now, and into eternity.

We come in gratitude and with such deep joy. Thank you for your gift of communion.

———— · ✳ · ————

When it was time, he sat down, all the apostles with him, and said, "You've no idea how much I have looked forward to eating this Passover meal with you before I enter my time of suffering. It's the last one I'll eat until we all eat it together in the kingdom of God."

Taking the cup, he blessed it, then said, "Take this and pass it among you. As for me, I'll not drink wine again until the kingdom of God arrives."

Taking bread, he blessed it, broke it, and gave it to them, saying, "This is my body, given for you. Eat it in my memory."

He did the same with the cup after supper, saying, "This cup is the new covenant written in my blood, blood poured out for you."[27]

—————— • ❈ • ——————

Lord, we count it such a privilege that you invite us to partake of your body and your blood. Jesus, as you said, "Unless you eat the flesh of the Son of Man and drink his blood, you have no life in you."[28]

We want your life. We eat and drink in gratitude. Thank you.

Savor Communion: Day 9
THE WORDS OF LIFE

Jesus, we think about how, early in your ministry, when you told the Jews that you were the true manna, the bread of life that came from heaven, and that they would need to eat your flesh and drink your blood, many turned back and didn't continue with you anymore.

"You do not want to leave too, do you?" Jesus asked the Twelve.

Simon Peter answered him, "Lord, to whom shall we go? You have the words of eternal life. We have come to believe and to know that you are the Holy One of God."[29]

Lord, we give thanks that not only do you give us your flesh and your blood to eat and drink, but we also thank you that you have the words of eternal life, and you share them with us.

Thank you, Jesus.

------ • ❋ • ------

For I received from the Lord what I also delivered to you, that the Lord Jesus on the night when he was betrayed took bread, and when he had given thanks, he broke it, and said, "This is my body, which is for you. Do this in remembrance of me." In the same way also he took the cup, after supper, saying, "This cup is the new covenant in my blood. Do this, as often as you drink it, in remembrance of me." For as often as you eat this bread and drink the cup, you proclaim the Lord's death until he comes.[30]

———— • ✸ • ————

Lord, we give you praise.

Thank you, Father. Thank you, Jesus. Thank you, Holy Spirit.

Lord, thank you for the beauty of your body. Thank you for the mystery of your blood, and for the power in Jesus' name.

We worship you, Lord. We give you glory. We give you honor.

As we eat and drink, we preach, declare, proclaim your death until you come.

Amen.

Savor Communion: Day 10
NUTRIENTS

Jesus, when you spoke to the woman at the well in John 4, she was a Samaritan, and therefore normally one the Jews would reject.

And she'd also been rejected and divorced by five husbands, until she gave up and cohabited with a sixth.

But to this rejected woman you offered yourself as living water. You gave her truth. And then she went out and became the first evangelist, and led her entire city to you.

As she went off to do that work, Lord, the disciples came back. And they urged you to eat, but you said, "I have food to eat that you know nothing about." And that word "food" in Aramaic means "nutrients."

Jesus, you were saying, "I have the sustenance needed to grow and maintain my life; I have all essential nourishment, because I do the work of my Father."

Jesus, thank you that you give us your body for food.

Thank you that you invite us to share in the food that the world knows nothing about.

Thank you that you invite us to join with you in your work of redeeming the world. You are so good to us, Lord.

———·✻·———

Now as they were eating, Jesus took bread, and after blessing it broke it and gave it to the disciples, and said, "Take, eat; this is my body." And he took a cup, and when he had given thanks he gave it to them, saying, "Drink of it, all of you, for this is my blood of the covenant, which is poured out for many for the forgiveness of sins."[31]

———— • ✸ • ————

Thank you, Lord, that you share your body. Thank you, Lord, for the power of your blood. Thank you that you break the curse and the shame, and that you empower us to victory.

As we walk in your ways, may our lives be a story of hope, of optimism, and of encouragement. We bless your name today, Lord Jesus. Thank you, Lord.

Savor Communion: Day 11
HEALING

Lord, the early church thought about healing both as a way to show love and compassion to those who were hurting, but also as a way demonstrate the truth of Jesus' claims.

Lord, when you saw the crowds, you always looked on them with love and compassion, and you would heal because your compassion would well up within you. You are so gracious.

Praise the Lord, my soul; all my inmost being, praise his holy name. Praise the Lord, my soul, and forget not all his benefits—who forgives all your sins and heals all your diseases, who redeems your life from the pit and crowns you with love and compassion, who satisfies your desires with good things so that your youth is renewed like the eagle's.[32]

Lord, when we eat your body and drink your blood, we are taking you, with your love and compassion, into ourselves. You, Jesus, whose very name means, "God heals; God saves."

Thank you that you forgive all our sins and heal all our diseases, that you redeem our lives from the pit and crown us with love and compassion.

———— • ✳ • ————

And as they were eating, he took bread, and after blessing

it broke it and gave it to them, and said, "Take; this is my body." And he took a cup, and when he had given thanks he gave it to them, and they all drank of it. And he said to them, "This is my blood of the covenant, which is poured out for many. Truly, I say to you, I will not drink again of the fruit of the vine until that day when I drink it new in the kingdom of God."[33]

———— • ✳ • ————

Lord, bless the bread and the cup. Lord, as we eat and drink, we welcome the supernatural partnership with our God.

Lord, we eat your body and drink your blood in this divine mystery.

May we enter into your cadence, your rhythm, your life.

Thank you, Lord. We remember your death and resurrection.

Savor Communion: Day 12
INEVITABILITY

Lord, your word is so beautiful:
As the rain and the snow
come down from heaven,
and do not return to it
without watering the earth
and making it bud and flourish,
so that it yields seed for the sower and bread for the eater,
so is my word that goes out from my mouth:
It will not return to me empty,
but will accomplish what I desire
and achieve the purpose for which I sent it.[34]

Lord, we read this and think of how a desert, after even a little rain, produces flowers, and how the more humid climates experience tremendous growth with the regular rains.

And if the rain and the snow don't return void, Lord, how much more your word. You bring to pass everything that you've purposed.

Your word goes forth and inevitably accomplishes all that it is supposed to.

Thank you that even the seed that gives the bread for the

eater is a picture of your will coming to pass. Thank you that your word is effectual.

————— • ❋ • —————

And when the hour came, he reclined at table, and the apostles with him. And he said to them, "I have earnestly desired to eat this Passover with you before I suffer. For I tell you I will not eat it until it is fulfilled in the kingdom of God." And he took a cup, and when he had given thanks he said, "Take this, and divide it among yourselves. For I tell you that from now on I will not drink of the fruit of the vine until the kingdom of God comes." And he took bread, and when he had given thanks, he broke it and gave it to them, saying, "This is my body, which is given for you. Do this in remembrance of me." And likewise the cup after they had eaten, saying, "This cup that is poured out for you is the new covenant in my blood. But behold, the hand of him who betrays me is with me on the table."[35]

————— • ❋ • —————

We praise you, Lord. We worship you. We pray that you bless the bread, bless the cup, as we eat in remembrance of you, as we drink in remembrance of you, as we participate, Lord, and partner with the mystery of your death and resurrection. Amen.

Savor Communion: Day 13
A BEAUTIFUL METAPHOR

Lord, we think about some of the different uses of wine throughout history.

Before Prohibition ended the home-grown fuel industry, Lord, some people used wine to run cars.

Before that, it was used for an anesthetic during surgery, to dull the senses and allow surgery to go on without the shock to the patient directly. Wine has been used for cleaning wounds. It has preserved certain types of food, like fruits, that wouldn't dry quickly enough in humid climates.

We think of how herbalists use wine to extract healing properties from plants in order to make tinctures, useful for healing.

Fermentation allowed farmers to preserve fresh grapes in an era before there was mass refrigeration—a way to store calories for the long-term.

And, of course, and most obviously, wine has always been good for the enlightening and enlivening of the spirit.

Lord, what a symbol to choose for your blood! Thank you, Lord, for your energy, your kindness, your cleansing, your preserving, your healing, your sustenance, and your joy.

———— • ✵ • ————

For I received from the Lord what I also passed on to you, that the Lord Jesus on the night in which he was betrayed took bread, and after he had given thanks he broke it and said, "This is my body, which is for you. Do this in remembrance of me." In the same way, he also took the cup after supper, saying, "This cup is the new covenant in my blood. Do this, every time you drink it, in remembrance of me." For every time you eat this bread and drink the cup, you proclaim the Lord's death until he comes.[36]

———— • ✱ • ————

Lord, we thank you for the bread, thank you for the cup. Bless them, Lord.

We eat and drink in remembrance of you, grateful for the forgiveness of sins. In Jesus' name. Amen.

Let's celebrate!

Savor Communion: Day 14
A CONTINUAL FEAST

Lord, your word says, "All the days of the afflicted are evil: but he that is of a merry heart hath a continual feast."[37]

And, Lord, the only way that we can have a life that is not afflicted with evil is to be in your presence. Thank you that you open the way.

And we might be tempted to read the second half of this proverb as saying, "Well, if you could just figure out how to generate a merry heart, then you could have a continual feast, but you can't, so bummer for you."

But the reality is: you give us the merry, cheerful heart, and so we receive the continual feast as a gift from you.

Thank you, Lord, too, that you allow us to walk in your joy, that you go before us as both the creator and the sustainer. You're the instigator and the one who brings it to fruition. The one who died, and who gives us his life. Thank you, Jesus.

———— · ✱ · ————

While they were eating, Jesus took bread, and after giving thanks he broke it, gave it to his disciples, and said, "Take, eat, this is my body." And after taking the cup and giving thanks, he gave it to them, saying, "Drink from it, all of you, for this is my blood, the blood of the covenant, that is poured out for many for the forgiveness of sins.[38]

———— • ✸ • ————

Lord, we hold the bread. We hold the cup. We think of your love overtaking us, of your goodness and lovingkindness pursuing us. We feel a deep longing in our heart for your love.

We celebrate your death and resurrection, and remember your gift.

Thank you, Lord. Amen.

Savor Communion: Day 15
THE PLEASURE OF EATING

Lord, what pleasure we find in the body working.
We recognize our five senses of sight, sound, smell, taste, and touch.

Lord, we recognize other, less well-known senses, such as *proprioception*, the ability to know where our bodies are in space; *empathy*, the ability to sense emotions (both ours and other people's); and *enteroception*, the ability to sense what we feel inside our bodies.

Lord, when we swallow the bread and the wine, we can feel them come into our bodies. And any time we have an interruption of eating, whether because of fasting, or some time on a liquid-only diet, the return to eating is such a specific, surprising pleasure.

Lord, thank you that you give us a picture that we get to take you into our mouths, and then that we have the sensation of the bread and the wine going down our esophagus to get to our stomach.

What a specific pleasure it is to eat something, and you share this pleasure with us. Thank you.

———— • ❈ • ————

While they were eating, he took bread, and after giving thanks he broke it, gave it to them, and said, "Take it. This is my body." And after taking the cup and giving thanks, he gave it to them, and they all drank from it. He said to them, "This is my blood, the blood of the covenant, that is poured out for many. I tell you the truth, I will no longer drink of the fruit of the vine until that day when I drink it new in the kingdom of God."[39]

———— • ❀ • ————

Lord Jesus, bless the bread and the wine and the miracle of the Lord's Table.

Lord, as we eat and drink, may there be a supernatural transference of your body and of your blood, in us and through us.

In Jesus' name. Amen.

Let's eat and celebrate!

Savor Communion: Day 16
MORE THAN CRUMBS

Lord, the Syrophoenician woman asked that her daughter be released from an evil spirit. And at first you refused her, which seems more than a little unkind.

"It is not right to take the children's bread and toss it to the dogs."

"Lord," she replied, "even the dogs under the table eat the children's crumbs."

Then he told her, "For such a reply, you may go; the demon has left your daughter."[40]

We stand amazed that even your crumbs carry such authority to heal. Even a crumb of you is powerful and effective.

And you don't give us crumbs!

Lord, we come to you with such gratitude that your power and authority are so great that quantity doesn't matter, and yet you give us your body, broken. You give us your blood, shed.

———·✸·———

Now when the hour came, Jesus took his place at the table and the apostles joined him. And he said to them, "I have earnestly desired to eat this Passover with you before I suffer.

For I tell you, I will not eat it again until it is fulfilled in the kingdom of God." Then he took a cup, and after giving thanks he said, "Take this and divide it among yourselves. For I tell you that from now on I will not drink of the fruit of the vine until the kingdom of God comes." Then he took bread, and after giving thanks he broke it and gave it to them, saying, "This is my body which is given for you. Do this in remembrance of me." And in the same way he took the cup after they had eaten, saying, "This cup that is poured out for you is the new covenant in my blood."[41]

———— • ✹ • ————

Lord, we take the bread, we take the cup, and we eat and drink in remembrance of you. We partake of your body, the divine mystery. In Jesus' name. Amen.

Let's eat and drink and celebrate.

Savor Communion: Day 17
TAKE A BIG SWIG

Lord, when Bob went to the Soviet Union in the early 1990s, the Pentecostal brothers, those dynamic apostolic leaders whose parents had been imprisoned, found the Lord's Table to be so powerful.

They would say to the congregation, "We drink from one cup, and we encourage you to take a big swig of the wine. Let it burn. Let it bring a burning!"

Lord, may your blood burn in us and bring a burning. Accomplish your purposes on the earth through us.

———— · ✳ · ————

I passed on to you the tradition the Lord gave to me: On the same night the Lord Jesus was betrayed, He took the bread *in His hands*; and after giving thanks *to God*, He broke it and said, "This is My body, *broken* for you. Keep doing this so that you *and all who come after* will have a vivid reminder of Me." After they had finished dinner, He took the cup and in the same way said, "This cup is the new covenant, *executed* in My blood. Keep doing this; and whenever you drink it, you *and all who come after* will have a vivid reminder of Me." Every time you taste this bread and every time you place the cup *to your mouths* and drink, you are declaring the Lord's death, *which is the ultimate expression of His faithfulness and love,* until He comes again.[42]

—————— • ❋ • ——————

Lord, we hold this bread and hold this cup in our hands and we look into your face. We see the smile of our Savior and King. As we prepare our hearts to eat and drink in remembrance of you, we acknowledge that you're with us. And we accept the mystery of communion.

We partake with you. Thank you.

Savor Communion: Day 18
NOURISHMENT

Lord, sometimes we come to you completely depleted. We go to sleep depleted, and we wake up exhausted, and each decision requires laborious processing.

Sometimes we feel like we have no strength left in our bodies.

Lord, in the midst of our fatigue, you nourish us. You give yourself to us as actual, literal food.

And, Lord, we think, too, about how, in John 4, you spoke peace and healing to the woman at the well, and when the disciples returned and urged you to eat, you said that you had food to eat that they knew nothing about.

Thank you, Jesus, that you give us both literal, physical food, and the figurative food, the soul satisfaction, that comes from doing the Father's will.

Thank you that you make provision for us, that you promise that our strength is renewed like the eagles', and that you refresh us in every way.

———— • ✻ • ————

As they were eating, Jesus took some bread. He offered a blessing *over the bread*, and then He broke it and gave it to His disciples.

Jesus: Take this and eat; it is My body.

And then He took the cup *of wine*, He made a blessing over it, and He passed it around the table.

Jesus: Take this and drink, all of you: this is My blood of the new covenant, which is poured out for many for the forgiveness of sins.[43]

——————•✹•——————

Lord, we want to remember your benefits. We think of how you look us in the eyes, with your love, your compassion, and your goodness, and you say, "This is my body. This is my blood."

Lord, we thank you for the miracle of the Table of the Lord.

We eat and drink in thanksgiving and celebration of you.

Hallelujah!

Savor Communion: Day 19
MAGNIFICAT

Jesus, when your mother knew she was bearing you, she praised you, and we join in her song:

My soul glorifies the Lord
and my spirit rejoices in God my Savior, ...
for the Mighty One has done great things for me—
holy is his name.
His mercy extends to those who fear him,
from generation to generation.
He has performed mighty deeds with his arm; ...
He has filled the hungry with good things....[44]

We do glorify you, Lord, and rejoice in you and the great things you have done for us.

And as we come to communion, we thank you that you have filled us, the hungry, with good things. With your flesh and blood, in fact. Thank you.

———— · ❋ · ————

As they ate, Jesus took bread, offered a blessing, and broke it. He handed the pieces to His disciples.

Jesus: Take this [and eat it]. This is My body.

He took a cup *of wine*; and when He had given thanks *for it*, He passed it to them, and they all drank from it.

Jesus: This is My blood, a covenant poured out on behalf of many. Truly I will never taste the fruit of the vine again until the day when I drink it new in the kingdom of God.[45]

———— •✺• ————

Lord, we welcome you. Lord, we praise you as we ponder the mystery of the Eucharist, the Table of the Lord.

Lord, as we hold the bread and the wine, we thank you that you invite us to partake of the body and blood of the Lord. Thank you, Jesus.

We proclaim your death again today, with gratitude and celebration. Thank you. Amen.

Savor Communion: Day 20
MYSTERY

Lord, I think about how C.S. Lewis, with all his wisdom and brilliance, yet found the Table of the Lord a mystery:

I don't know and can't imagine what the disciples understood our Lord to mean when, His body still unbroken and His blood unshed, He handed them the bread and wine, saying they were His body and blood.... They are, on the natural level, such a very odd symbol of that.... Yet I find no difficulty in believing that the veil between the worlds, nowhere else (for me) so opaque to the intellect, is nowhere else so thin and permeable to divine operation. Here a hand from the hidden country touches not only my soul but my body.... Here is big medicine and strong magic.... The command, after all, was Take, eat: not Take, understand.[46]

Thank you, Jesus, that you say, "Take, eat."

We do so, in the midst of the mystery.

———— • ❋ • ————

When the meal was prepared, Jesus sat at the table, joined by His emissaries.

Jesus: It has been My deep desire to eat this Passover meal with you before My suffering begins. Know this: I will not eat another Passover meal until its meaning is fulfilled in the kingdom of God.

He took a cup *of wine* and gave thanks for it.

Jesus: Take this; share it among yourselves. Know this: I will not drink another sip of wine until the kingdom of God has arrived in fullness.

Then He took bread, gave thanks, broke it, and shared it with them.

Jesus: This is My body, My body given for you. Do this to remember Me.

And similarly, after the meal had been eaten, He took the cup.

Jesus: This cup, which is poured out for you, is the new covenant, made in My blood.[47]

—————— • ✸ • ——————

Lord, we come as partakers of the supernatural mystery. With the bread and the wine, we hold the beauty of the Lord and the splendor of our King. We put our trust in you again this day, and say thank you.

Amen.

We eat and drink in celebration. Thank you, Lord!

Savor Communion: Day 21
FEEDING PEOPLE

Lord God, we think about how often, in the scriptures, you fed people.

- The Israelites in the wilderness for 40 years ate manna from heaven.
- The prophet Elijah by the brook ate the food brought every day by ravens.
- The besieged Samaritans miraculously enjoyed abundance, as Elisha prophesied.[48]
- Jesus multiplied the food and fed the 5000.
- Then did the same miracle with the 4000.

And then we think of you, Jesus, feeding your disciples at the Last Supper, and then, again, on the day of your resurrection, how you walked with two on the road to Emmaus, and then took bread, blessed, and broke it.

Thank you that you have fed your people through the ages, so that when you wanted a picture of your body, broken, you offered us food. How precious, Lord.

Thank you that you continue to feed us today.

———— • ❋ • ————

For I received from the Lord that which I also delivered to you, that the Lord Jesus, on the night when He was betrayed, took bread; and when He had given thanks, He broke it and said, "This is My body, which is for you; do this in remembrance of Me." In the same way *He* also *took* the cup after supper, saying, "This cup is the new covenant in My blood; do this, as often as you drink *it*, in remembrance of Me." For as often as you eat this bread and drink the cup, you proclaim the Lord's death until He comes.[49]

———— ·✱· ————

Lord, we thank you for this holy moment, a moment where, Jesus, you change us. Thank you for this moment of uniting our hearts. Thank you that we're one with you. We eat in remembrance of you. Amen.

Savor Communion: Day 22
FINEST WHEAT

Lord, we think about how wheat comes in different types, like red or white; how it comes in different varieties, like regular or spelt or einkorn; how it comes in different qualities, based on how uniformly the grains dry and how healthy the soil was in which the plants grew.

All of these different properties. And John Michael Talbot wrote the song "Gift of Finest Wheat," that says:

> *You satisfy the hungry heart*
> *With gift of finest wheat*
> *Come give to us, O Saving Lord*
> *The Bread of Life to eat*[50]

Lord, thank you for the picture of you as the finest wheat: crushed on our behalf, then turned to bread and given to us for our sustenance, and for our remembrance.

Lord, we thank you.

———— • ✳ • ————

Now while they were eating, Jesus took *some* bread, and after a blessing, He broke *it* and gave *it* to the disciples, and said, "Take, eat; this is My body." And when He had taken a cup and given thanks, He gave *it* to them, saying, "Drink from it, all of you; for this is My blood of the covenant, which is being poured out for many for forgiveness of sins.[51]

————— • ✳ • —————

Lord Jesus, we take the bread. We agree with the psalmist who wrote, "He grants peace to your borders and satisfies you with the finest of wheat."[52]

You are that gift of finest wheat, Lord. Thank you.

Lord, we thank you for the cup. We think of your sacrifice, your love, your intimacy, your friendship, your commitment to us. Thank you, Lord.

Please bless the bread and the cup as we eat and drink.

In Jesus' name. Amen.

Savor Communion: Day 23
CAPTURED

Lord, we think of how, during the Last Supper, you gave both a solid and a liquid.

The bread needs no receptacle.

But the wine needs the cup to contain it.

Thank you, Jesus, that you had a body that contained your blood.

And thank you, Lord, for the picture in the Old Testament of the Passover lamb, whose blood was caught in the basin so it could be applied to the doorframes of the houses. Thank you that the cup represents that basin, that your blood continues to be captured and held for us.

Thank you, Lord, that you gave your blood freely for the remission of sins. And we thank you that your gifts are irrevocable.

Thank you that we get to apply the blood.

Thank you that your blood cleanses us from all sin.

———— ·✸· ————

While they were eating, He took *some* bread, and after a blessing He broke *it*, and gave *it* to them, and said, "Take *it*; this is My body." And when He had taken a cup *and* given thanks, He gave *it* to them, and they all drank from it. And He said to them, "This is My blood of the covenant, which is being poured out for many. Truly I say to you, I will not drink of the fruit of the vine again, until that day when I drink it, new, in the kingdom of God."[53]

——————•❋•——————

Lord, we thank you for the gifts of God. For the Table, the love, the beauty of the body and the blood of Jesus Christ. Thank you, Lord.

We take the bread, we take the cup, with rejoicing and with gratitude.

In the name of Jesus. Amen.

Savor Communion: Day 24
ONENESS

Lord Jesus, during the Last Supper, you prayed to the Father on behalf of the disciples and all who believe through their message, "That all of them may be one, Father, just as you are in me and I am in you. May they also be in us so that the world may believe that you have sent me. I have given them the glory that you gave me, that they may be one as we are one—I in them and you in me—so that they may be brought to complete unity. Then the world will know that you sent me and have loved them even as you have loved me."[54]

You give us an astonishing invitation to unity with you and the Father. The Father is in you, and then you give us your body to eat.

Thank you that, because of this unity, the world believes in you, Jesus.

And, even better, know that you have loved them, even as the Father loves the Son. Astonishing. Amazing.

———— • ✻ • ————

When the hour came, He reclined *at the table*, and the apostles with Him. And He said to them, "I have eagerly desired to eat this Passover with you before I suffer; for I say to you, I shall not eat it *again* until it is fulfilled in the kingdom of God." And when He had taken a cup *and* given thanks, He said, "Take this and share it among yourselves; for I say to you, I will not drink of the fruit of the vine from now on until the kingdom of God comes." And when He had taken *some* bread *and* given thanks, He broke it and gave it to them, saying, "This is My body, which is being given for you; do this in remembrance of Me." And in the same way *He took* the cup after they had eaten, saying, "This cup, which is poured out for you, is the new covenant in My blood.[55]

———— • ✸ • ————

Jesus, as you took the bread, we can picture you, with the disciples around you. We sense the warmth, the vitality, the light and the love coming from you.

Lord, we look into your face today as we take the bread and partake of your flesh, as we take the cup and partake of your blood.

Thank you.

Savor Communion: Day 25
REMAIN

Lord Jesus, you said, "Remain in me, as I also remain in you. No branch can bear fruit by itself; it must remain in the vine. Neither can you bear fruit unless you remain in me. I am the vine; you are the branches. If you remain in me and I in you, you will bear much fruit; apart from me you can do nothing."[56]

You ask us to remain in you, or, as some translations say, *abide*.

And no branch of a grape vine grips the vine with white-knuckled fear. The branch simply grows: no straining, no gripping, no grasping.

The branch lives as part of the whole.

Teach us to abide. Teach us to remain.

———— • ✳ • ————

For I received from the Lord Himself that [instruction] which I passed on to you, that the Lord Jesus on the night in which He was betrayed took bread; and when He had given thanks, He broke it and said, "This is (represents) My body, which is [offered as a sacrifice] for you. Do this in [affectionate] remembrance of Me." In the same way, after supper *He took* the cup, saying, "This cup is the new covenant [ratified and established] in My blood; do this, as often as you drink it, in [affectionate] remembrance of Me." For every time you eat this bread and drink this cup, you are [symbolically] proclaiming [the fact of] the Lord's death until He comes [again].[57]

———— • ✱ • ————

Lord, you said, "I am the bread of life. Whoever comes to me will never go hungry, and whoever believes in me will never be thirsty."[58]

And then you said, "I am the true vine."[59]

You are both the bread and the wine. We eat and drink in remembrance of you. Amen.

Savor Communion: Day 26
ANGUISH

Jesus, thank you that you willingly share yourself with us so generously.

You didn't say, "My intimate relationship with the Father is perfect and unblemished and has existed since before time began. I'd rather keep that perfect record intact."

Instead, you gave up your unbroken connection for us. You endured some level of separation from the Father, so that we would not have to.

"My God, my God, why have you forsaken me? Why are you so far from saving me, so far from my cries of anguish? But you, Lord, do not be far from me. You are my strength; come quickly to help me."[60]

Jesus, you chose to go through that agony. The physical pain must have been beyond describing, but the agony of feeling forsaken from the Father—Jesus, we can't comprehend it, because we have no context for it.

And we never will.

Thank you, Jesus, for bearing that burden. We are grateful.

And, Father, thank you that the same Psalm that prophesied Jesus' death also includes this truth about you: "For he has not despised or scorned the suffering of the afflicted one; he has not hidden his face from him but has listened to his cry for help."[61]

Thank you that though Jesus *felt* forsaken, the Psalm proclaims the truth: you did not despise him, nor hide your face from him.

We agree with the Psalmist and say: "He has done it!"[62]

———— • ✿ • ————

Now as they were eating Jesus took bread, and after blessing it, He broke it and gave it to the disciples, and said, "Take, eat; this is My body." And when He had taken a cup and given thanks, He gave it to them, saying, "Drink from it, all of you; for this is My blood of the [new and better] covenant, which [ratifies the agreement and] is being poured out for many [as a substitutionary atonement] for the forgiveness of sins.[63]

———— • ✿ • ————

Lord Jesus, we are so humbled and so grateful. You are generous, generous, generous. You are always the greater King, always the one who gives more.

Thank you for giving your body and your blood.

We take and eat in remembrance of you.

Savor Communion: Day 27
JOY

Lord Jesus, Psalm 45 speaks of the bridegroom marrying his bride, a beautiful picture of you and the church. It says, speaking prophetically of you, "You love righteousness and hate wickedness; therefore God, your God, has set you above your companions by anointing you with the oil of joy."[64]

So even though the Table of the Lord remembers a sober, horrific event, so often we come with a sense of an upwelling of joy, invited to feast with the bridegroom.

Thank you for the invitation to feast!

Lord, a feast needs feasters, and we think of how you chose your disciples, and how much you enjoyed being with those chosen ones, your friends.

And we thank you that you like being with us, too. You like communing with us.

Thank you for the invitation to relationship!

———— • ✷ • ————

While they were eating, Jesus took bread and blessed it [giving thanks and praise], and He broke it, and gave it to them and said, "Take it. This is My body." And when He had taken a cup [of wine] and given thanks, He gave it to them, and they all drank from it. And He said to them, "This is My blood of the [new] covenant, [My blood] which is being poured out for many [for the forgiveness of sins]. I assure you *and* most solemnly say to you, I will not drink again of the fruit of the vine until that day when I drink it new in the kingdom of God."[65]

———— • ✳ • ————

Lord, we acknowledge you in the middle of this time. We see your face and celebrate your goodness and your love for us. Thank you, Jesus. We remember your death and your resurrection, and we celebrate you.

Savor Communion: Day 28
EUCHARIST

Lord Jesus, your Table is sometimes called "the Eucharist," from the Greek word that means "give thanks."

As Paul said: "And when he had given thanks [eucharisteo], he broke it and said, 'This is my body, which is for you; do this in remembrance of me."[66]

We think of how you gave thanks as you took the bread and the cup. You thanked God and served your disciples.

Now we come and we give thanks to you for communion, for the Eucharist.

We give thanks for the Giving Thanks.

Your word tells us to enter your gates with thanksgiving and your courts with praise. We come with the Eucharist.

———— •❋• ————

When the hour [for the meal] had come, Jesus reclined *at the table*, and the apostles with Him. He said to them, "I have earnestly wanted to eat this Passover with you before I suffer; for I say to you, I will not eat it again until it is fulfilled in the kingdom of God." And when He had taken a cup and given thanks, He said, "Take this and share it among yourselves; for I say to you, I will not drink of the fruit of the vine from

now on until the kingdom of God comes." And when He
had taken bread and given thanks, He broke it and gave it to
them, saying, "This is My body which is given for you; do this
in remembrance of Me." And in the same way *He took* the cup
after they had eaten, saying, "This cup, which is poured out
for you, is the new covenant [ratified] in My blood.[67]

———————— • ❋ • ————————

Lord, we take the bread and the cup, and we hold them in
our hands, these hands that have been set apart for you.

We ask that, whatever we do this day, that the anointing of
God would flow through our body, through our hands, and
through our voice.

And so, Lord, we eat this bread and drink this cup, in
remembrance of you.

Savor Communion: Day 29
GREATNESS

Lord Jesus, after you shared the Passover meal with your disciples, "A dispute also arose among them as to which of them was considered to be greatest,"[68] apparently a rather frequent topic of discussion among them.

How striking, Lord, that you didn't say, "Excuse me! Don't try to be great!"

Rather, you simply taught them what greatness looks like in your kingdom: not to lord it over others, but to serve.

We think about Mary, too, in her Magnificat. She didn't say, "Oh, from now on, everybody will completely forget about me because they'll be just so enthralled with the Lord." Rather she said, "From now on all generations will call me blessed."[69]

Lord, we, too, want to be great, as you define greatness.

————·✱·————

I have handed down to you what came to me by direct revelation from the Lord himself. The same night in which he was handed over, he took bread and gave thanks. Then he distributed it to the disciples and said, "Take it and eat your fill. It is my body, which is given for you. Do this to remember me." He did the same with the cup *of wine* after supper and said, "This cup seals the new covenant with my blood. Drink it—and whenever you drink this, do it to remember me."

Whenever you eat this bread and drink this cup, you are retelling the story, proclaiming our Lord's death until he comes.[70]

———— ·❋· ————

Lord, we thank you for the blessing of the bread. Thank you for the blessing of the cup. Thank you for the newness of life, the new covenant, the forgiveness of sins. Thank you that all condemnation, all shame, all guilt must go.

We thank you for the power of God to bring healing.

We want you to receive all glory, honor, and praise.

Thank you, Father. Thank you Jesus. We drink in remembrance of the covenant you made with us.

In Jesus' name. Amen.

Savor Communion: Day 30
EXPANSION

Lord, we cry out for more of you. We don't want to be stagnant in any way. We want your kingdom to advance. We want your harvest to be gathered in. We want our minds to fill with more of you, our days to be ever closer to you.

As creator and sustainer of the universe, please give us more. Prepare our hearts for the mystery of the Lord.

As we come to the Table of the Lord, we ask for a supernatural refilling, a supernatural refueling, supernatural help.

We want more spiritually, relationally, intellectually.

We want more faith, more hope, more love. More righteousness, peace, and joy in the Holy Spirit.

Thank you, Lord, that you fill us.

———— •❋• ————

As they ate, Jesus took the bread and blessed it and broke it and gave it to his disciples. He said to them, "This is my body. Eat it." Then taking the cup of wine, he gave thanks to the Father, he entered into covenant with them, saying, "This is my blood. Each of you must drink it in fulfillment of the covenant. For this is the blood that seals the new covenant. It will be poured out for many for the complete forgiveness of sins.[71]

———— • ✸ • ————

Lord, thank you for the bread, thank you for this cup. Bless this bread, in Jesus' name. Bless this cup.

Jesus, thank you for intimacy with you, union with you, identity and new purpose found in you, the wisdom and revelation and discernment found in you.

Lord, we eat and drink in Jesus' name, proclaiming your death, proclaiming your resurrection, and proclaiming that you are coming again.

Thank you, Lord.

Let's eat and drink and celebrate!

Savor Communion: Day 31
BLESSING

Lord, you tell us to bear one another's burdens. We recognize that men and women all over the world are in some very difficult places.

We pray, Lord, for our brothers and sisters. We pray for miracles in their lives. We ask for all the benefits you promise:
who forgives all your sins
and heals all your diseases,
who redeems your life from the pit
and crowns you with love and compassion,
who satisfies your desires with good things
so that your youth is renewed like the eagle's.
The Lord works righteousness
and justice for all the oppressed.[72]
As we take the bread, as we take the cup, Lord, we speak hope. We speak life.

Come, Holy Spirit. Move mightily. May the umbrella of your covering and your protection be on us.

Thank you that you have made us alive in Christ, part of the family of God.

Thank you, Lord.

———— •❋• ————

As they were dining, Jesus took the bread and blessed it, and broke it, and gave it to his disciples. He said to them, "Receive this; it is my body." Then taking the cup of wine and giving thanks to the Father, he declared the new covenant with them. And as each one drank from the cup, he said to them, "This is my blood, which seals the new covenant poured out for many. I tell you the truth, I will not drink again of the fruit of the vine until the day comes when we drink it together in the kingdom *feast* of my Father."[73]

——————— • ✳ • ———————

Lord, we take the bread and we take the wine.

We proclaim your death, your burial, and your resurrection. Great and mighty are you.

Thank you that you sent us the Holy Spirit to teach us all things.

Lord, we ponder how much you love us as we think about the Table of the Lord.

Lord, thank you for your body. Thank you for your blood.

We eat and drink, in Jesus' name. Amen.

EPILOGUE

How beautiful, that the Lord chooses to come and eat and fellowship with us.

In Don Richardson's *Peace Child*, he shares the story of living with the Sawi people of Papua New Guinea. Before the gospel came, the Sawi's highest goal was to trick someone into thinking that they were close friends, close enough eat together ... and then one would kill the other.

This cultural pattern ran so deep, when they first heard the story of Jesus, they thought that Judas was the hero. After all, he had lived as Jesus' friend, then betrayed him to his death.

The Sawi's sense of right and wrong was completely backwards.

Until the gospel came.

Fifty years later, Don Richardson returned for a visit.[74]

He noticed that some people had grey hair. "When I first came, there were no old people. They would all kill each other."

The gospel carries astonishing power to transform.

The invitation remains to come and dine.

God continues to extend fellowship.

And so, as you go out into the world this day and every day, you have the invitation to fellowship.

We invite you to continue to proclaim the Lord's death

until he comes.

We invite you to revisit these readings again and again.

Don't stop proclaiming the Lord's death, just because the month is over.

———————— • ✱ • ————————

When Jesus arrived at the upper room, he took his place at the table along with all the apostles. Then he told them, "I have longed with passion and desire to eat this Passover lamb with you before I endure my sufferings. I promise you that the next time we eat this, we will be together in the feast of God's kingdom."

Then he raised a cup and gave thanks to God and said to them, "Take this and pass it on to one another and drink. I promise you that the next time we drink this wine, we will be together in the feast of God's kingdom."

Then he lifted up a loaf, and after praying a prayer of thanksgiving to God, he gave each of his apostles a piece of bread, saying, "This loaf is my body, which is now being offered to you. Always eat it to remember me."

After supper was over, he lifted the cup again and said, "This cup is my blood of the new covenant I make with you, and it will be poured out soon for all of you.[75]

———————— • ✱ • ————————

Lord, we pray, "Thy kingdom come, thy will be done on earth as it is in heaven."

Your kingdom, Lord, of righteousness, peace and joy in the Holy Spirit.[76]

We welcome the fruit of the Spirit, the gift of the Lord.

We welcome your resurrection power through us.

Thank you. Amen.

NOTES

1 Ephesians 6:12
2 Remember how the word "angel" means "messenger"? See the word angel in the Greek?
3 I Corinthians 11:29-30
4 I Corinthians 11:23-26
5 Thank you to my MacBook's computer dictionary.
6 https://en.wikipedia.org/wiki/Divine_grace. Found 12/26/2021.
7 I Corinthians 11:17-34
8 Galatians 2:20 and others
9 Matthew 19:13-15
10 Psalm 127:3
11 II Timothy 2:13
12 I Corinthians 11:23-26 NIV
13 I Peter 2:4-5
14 James 1:17
15 Matthew 26:26-28 NIV
16 Mark 14:22-25 NIV
17 Luke 22:14-21 NIV
18 John 2:1-12
19 I Corinthians 11:23-26 MSG
20 Matthew 26:26-28 MSG
21 Mark 14:22-25 MSG
22 Romans 5:9
23 Ephesians 1:7
24 I John 1:7
25 Ephesians 2:13
26 Revelation 12:11
27 Luke 22:14-20 MSG
28 John 6:53
29 John 6:67-69
30 I Corinthians 11:23-26 ESV
31 Matthew 26:26-28 ESV
32 Psalm 103:1-5
33 Mark 14:22-25 ESV
34 Isaiah 55:10-11
35 Luke 22:14-21 ESV
36 I Corinthians 11:23-26 NET
37 Proverbs 15:15 KJV
38 Matthew 26:26-28 NET
39 Mark 14:22-25 NET
40 Mark 7:24-30
41 Luke 22:14-20 NET
42 I Corinthians 11:23-26 VOICE
43 Matthew 26:26-28 VOICE
44 Luke 1:46-53
45 Mark 14:22-25 VOICE
46 C.S. Lewis, Letters to Malcolm, https://www.davidlose.net/2013/03/c-s-lewis-on-holy-communion/. Found 12/27/2021.
47 Luke 22:14-20 VOICE
48 II Kings 6-7
49 I Corinthians 11:23-26 NASB
50 http://www.songlyrics.com/john-michael-talbot/gift-of-finest-wheat-lyrics/. Found 12/27/2021.
51 Matthew 26:26-28 NASB
52 Psalm 147:14
53 Mark 14:22-25 NASB
54 John 17:20-23
55 Luke 22:14-20 NASB
56 John 15:4-5
57 I Corinthians 11:23-26 AMP
58 John 6:35
59 John 15:1
60 Psalm 22:1, 19
61 Psalm 22:23
62 Psalm 22:31
63 Matthew 26:26-28 AMP
64 Psalm 45:7
65 Mark 14:22-25 AMP
66 I Corinthians 11:24
67 Luke 22:14-20 AMP

68 Luke 22:24

69 Luke 1:48

70 1 Corinthians 11:23-26 TPT

71 Matthew 26:26-28 TPT

72 Psalm 103:3-6

73 Mark 14:22-25

74 See Never the Same, at https:// youtu.be/mm6R9EPtMHo

75 Luke 22:14-20 TPT

76 Romans 14:17

ABOUT THE AUTHORS

Bob Perry has been a passionate student of prayer for more than four decades, constantly asking, "Lord, teach me to pray." He has founded and led multiple prayer initiatives that have trained and mobilized hundreds of thousands of people in prayer partnerships.

Amy Joy Lykosh loves healing and deliverance. Her heart's cry comes from the verse, "My people are destroyed for lack of knowledge" (Hosea 4:6). The author of several highly acclaimed books, she seeks to stop the destruction as best she can through writing and speaking.

Together, they run Workplace Prayer, to cover businesses in prayer, and Prayer Mentoring, to raise up healthy intercessors to bring the kingdom of God to bear in their lives and communities.

THE PRINCE PROTECTS HIS CITY

Nehemiah Prayed Four Months, Then Rebuilt the Wall in Only 52 Days

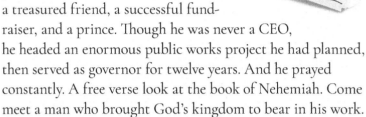

Such a great story! But how easy to miss!

Nehemiah wasn't a warrior or a king. He was a tremendous administrator, a gifted leader, a world-class historian, a treasured friend, a successful fundraiser, and a prince. Though he was never a CEO, he headed an enormous public works project he had planned, then served as governor for twelve years. And he prayed constantly. A free verse look at the book of Nehemiah. Come meet a man who brought God's kingdom to bear in his work.

"I finished reading it today! Loved it. Such a nice quick pace to read Nehemiah and also space to sit in parts if I just wanted to read one page" — **Angela**

FIND OUT MORE AT   **ORDER AT**
makariospress.com/the-prince-protects-his-city   **amazon.com**

GROW WITH PRAYER EXPERIENCES

Throughout the year, we offer a wide range of prayer experiences: Communal Fasts, Prayer Challenges, and Sacred Assemblies.

If you want to grow in prayer in creative and unexpected ways, come join us.

FIND OUT MORE AT
PrayerExperiences.com

ONE VOICE: THE STORY OF WILLIAM WILBERFORCE
Gorgeous Story of Tenacity + Courage

Biography in verse of the man who, despite all obstacles, fought to end the Slave Trade in Great Britain. Powerful story of tenacity and courage.

> "I think it's important to know Wilberforce's story, but One Voice has become one of my absolute favourite books of all time and is SO worth buying just for the beautiful writing. I was so skeptical when I first opened it and realized it was written in free verse but oh, it's so, so special. I can't make it through without sobbing." — **Emily**

ORDER EXCLUSIVELY AT
sonlight.com

---

21 DAYS OF A F(E)AST
A Fast That Feels More Like a Feast

Why fasting is a joy, and why you should do it. A guide for a fast that anyone can do, even if you can't restrict calories. The four types of fasting, and how to choose. Morning and evening readings for 21 days. Stories and testimonies. Drawn from four decades of experience and wisdom. Come sit in the Lord's presence.

> "Appreciating the wealth within this book!! Such a brilliant resource!" — **Nicole**

ORDER AT
amazon.com

PRAYER REFRESH
Short Prayers to Pray Through Your Day

You don't have to completely change your life, your habits, your personality, or your social media usage in order to have a good prayer life.

This book introduces a wide variety of prayers that you can pray in a minute or less, that will fit into your day, right where you are. Don't start with hours on your knees. Start with the stray half minutes here and there. Use it as a devotional for 21 days, or read straight through.

> "The Prayer Refresh was so life changing, perspective shattering, and breathed so much, much needed life into me and our home that I long to go through it again. Regularly. Like monthly." — **Amanda**

ORDER AT
amazon.com

JUNETEENTH: AN INVITATION TO FAST
Both the Why and the How To

Join us in a one-day fast.

> "The booklet was so helpful with the historical summary of the date (which I knew nothing about), as well as specific prayers and family examples, to guide my focused petitions. The format is beautiful, and so clearly organized! Great resource!" — **Eileen**

ORDER AT
amazon.com